Mr. Pepperpot

Written by Gwen Pascoe
Illustrated by Dianne Vanderee

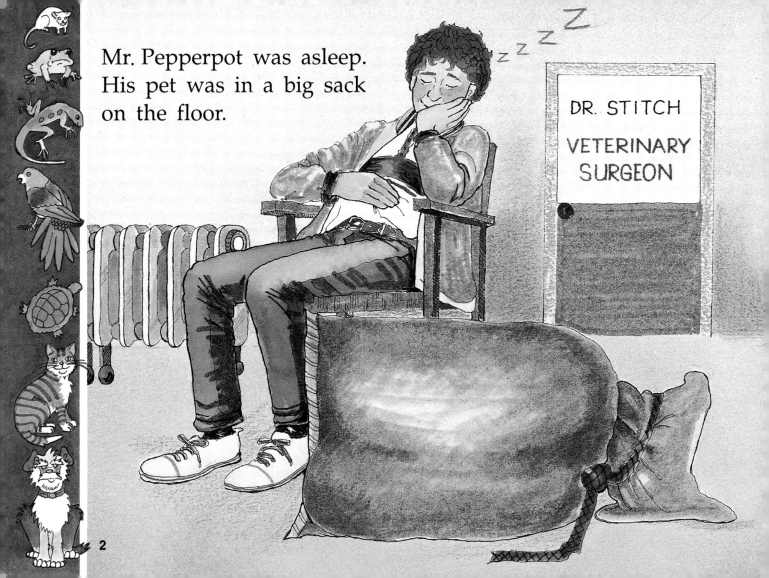

Mr. Pepperpot was asleep.
His pet was in a big sack
on the floor.

DR. STITCH

VETERINARY
SURGEON

2

In came Mrs. Loodledoodle
with her pet in a bucket.

She looked at the big sack on
the floor next to Mr. Pepperpot,
and she wondered
what on earth
could be in it.

Mrs. Loodledoodle's pet
rustled in its bucket,
but the big sack on the floor
didn't move or make a sound.

RUSTLE

RUSTLE

3

In came Mr. Collywobble
with his pet in a box.

He looked at the big sack on
the floor next to Mr. Pepperpot,
and he wondered
what could possibly
be in it.

Mr. Collywobble's pet
scratched inside the box,
but the big sack on the floor
didn't move or make a sound.

scratch

scratch

5

In came Mrs. Muddleberry
with her pet in a glove.

She looked at the big sack
on the floor next to
Mr. Pepperpot,
and she wondered
what on earth
could be in it.

Mrs. Muddleberry's pet
squeaked in the glove,
but the big sack on
the floor didn't move
or make a sound.

In came Mr. Tiddlewink
with his pet in a plastic bowl.

He looked at the big sack on
the floor next to Mr. Pepperpot,
and he wondered
what could possibly
be in it.

8

Mr. Tiddlewink's pet scraped at the sides of the bowl, but the big sack on the floor didn't move or make a sound.

SCRAPE

SCRAPE

In came Mrs. Fooglefum
with her pet in a jar.

She looked at the big sack on
the floor next to Mr. Pepperpot,
and she wondered
what on earth
could be in it.

Mrs. Fooglefum's pet
croaked in the jar,
but the big sack on
the floor didn't move
or make a sound.

In came Mr. Pifflesniff
with his pet in a cage.

He looked at the big sack on
the floor next to Mr. Pepperpot,
and he wondered
what could possibly
be in it.

Mr. Pifflesniff's pet squawked in the cage, but the big sack on the floor didn't move or make a sound.

squawk

squawk

In came Mr. Dragalong's pet,
pulling Mr. Dragalong behind it.

Mr. Dragalong looked at
the big sack on the floor.

"What's in there?" he said.

Mr. Dragalong's pet pushed its nose against the sack and sniffed. Then it barked, "WOOF! WOOF! WOOF!"

sniff
sniff

"SSHHH!" said everyone.
"SSSSS!" said the sack,
and it moved.

Then everything happened at once.

Mrs. Loodledoodle's lizard leaped from the bucket.

It ran across Mr. Collywobble's feet and slithered under the heater.

Mr. Collywobble's cat howled and clawed its way out of the box.

It scrambled onto Mrs. Fooglefum's shoulders and climbed up the curtains.

Mrs. Fooglefum's frog jumped
out of the jar.

It hopped high in the air
and landed in the fishtank.

Mr. Tiddlewink's tortoise tumbled out of the bowl and tried to hide in Mrs. Muddleberry's handbag.

Mrs. Muddleberry dropped the glove and her mouse ran across the floor and up Mr. Pifflesniff's leg.

The door of the cage broke open and Mr. Pifflesniff's parrot flew out.

It squawked as it flew around the room, and then it landed on top of the heater.

Mr. Collywobble's cat tried to catch the parrot.

Mr. Dragalong's dog tried to catch the cat.

21

The sack moved again.
"SSSSS!" it said,
and Mr. Pepperpot
finally woke up.

Just then the vet opened the door.

"What noisy pets!" he said.
"Now, who's first?"

He looked at his list.

"Ah, yes. Mr. Pepperpot's
python, please."

"So **that's** what's in the sack!"
said everyone.

DR. STITCH

23

Mr. Pepperpot carried his pet out of the waiting room.

"SSSSS!" it said.